Advance Praise

"Whether you're longing to recapture your old spark or you're a forty-something comfortable in your own skin, this book has so much to offer. In an era of selfies, social media, and porn-on-demand, how do we shut out the noise affecting our self-image and connect with who we are and what we want? This is the poignant discussion Erica guides us through in this book. It provides answers to questions we didn't know we were asking."

— **Erin Lyon**, Romantic Comedy Author

"This book is pure delight! I recommend putting on some classic French music and sipping a lovely cold glass of champagne as you read. A real treat."

— **Veronica Masters**, Instructional Design

"I found Erica's writing approachable, honest, and frankly resonating for me. And, made me more curious to the full 'Sexy Again Method.'"

— **Jenny Cretu**, COO, medical practice

"Everything [in this book] resonated with me. A self-help book I want to read over and over. It's relevant at multiple times throughout life. I think a group exercise would be amazing: a setting of 'how do I make me feel better vs. a husband bashing session.' There are so many women who NEED this book! It's wonderful."

— **Amy Jo Moore**, Mechanical Engineering Department Manager

"[*Feel Sexy Again*] is excellent! Easy to read, to the point, clear guidance and most importantly – motivational. I loved it!"

— **Lisa Ballard**, Senior Advisor, medical industry

"She nailed it! Erica gives the readers the tools to love themselves, take inventory of what's important, and take a leap of faith…loved the book!"

— **Jill Miler**, Integration Manager, medical practice

Feel Sexy Again

FEEL
sexy again

THE ULTIMATE GUIDE
TO RECLAIMING
YOUR SEXUAL CONFIDENCE

ERICA LEMKE-PEMBROKE, MA

NEW YORK

LONDON • NASHVILLE • MELBOURNE • VANCOUVER

Feel Sexy Again

The Ultimate Guide to Reclaiming Your Sexual Confidence

Published in New York, New York, by Morgan James Publishing in partnership with Difference Press. Morgan James is a trademark of Morgan James, LLC. www.MorganJamesPublishing.com

ISBN 9781642799248 paperback
ISBN 9781642799255 eBook
ISBN 9781642799262 audio
Library of Congress Control Number: 2019955622

Cover Design Concept: Jennifer Stimson

Cover Design: Megan Dillon megan@creativeninjadesigns.com

Interior Design: Chris Treccani www.3dogcreative.net

Editor: Cory Hott

Book Coaching: The Author Incubator

Morgan James is a proud partner of Habitat for Humanity Peninsula and Greater Williamsburg. Partners in building since 2006.

Get involved today! Visit
MorganJamesPublishing.com/giving-back

To my soul sisters.

You know who you are.

Table of Contents

Foreword

We live in strange times. People drive a few miles to work out in a gym, pop out of the car and take the escalator to the front door. We buy pills to help us sleep and pills to help us get going. Celebrities are famous for being famous. Photoshopped rich girls are the movers and shakers of fashion and glamor.

It seems that many of us have forgotten one of the foundations of western civilization: we are mind, body, soul, and spirit. These aren't four distinct parts, places or map directions. We are not a collection of parts; we are beautifully one piece.

We forget this at our peril.

Erica Lemke-Pembroke's new work, *Feel Sexy Again*, challenges us to rethink our relationship with ourselves. From pink wigs to training with kettlebells, ELP shares her story, and the stories of many clients, in her search to reawaken that passion for life…the juice of life.

Transparency is crucial in discussing the role of sex in life and Erica is sliding glass door here. Her work includes honest insights about raising a daughter in this new world of social media and dealing with the issues that come with raising "our beautiful little leeches." She is honest about porn and porn culture and the benefits of taking strip classes (S-Factor).

But this is what we need. We need women to come forward and share their stories. We need to hear the joys and sorrows of life and living…and how to return to the path, the journey, to a satisfied life.

Absolutely, sex is part of this journey. ELP is clear about this throughout the book. But, of course, there is more. She shares her core values of intimacy, safety and fitness. She admits that choosing these three surprised her at first, but her path to both her own transformation and her clients seem to hang on these three pillars.

Erica's personal journey back to sexy includes an interesting change in her approach to fitness and health. She shares with us:

I ate better. I ate my veggies. I ate real food (like an adult) and drank water. I stopped drinking. I re-started my stretching and kettlebell strength programs.

I danced again. I meditated again. I connected with friends. I slept better. And I asked for help. I went to my doctor to get some much overdue blood work, including a hormonal balance check. I found out that I not only had high familial cholesterol but that I also had almost zero testosterone in my body. As a perimenopausal woman, I still need this important hormone to function normally. Stress was the predominant factor in this hormone imbalance. And after being given my options, I decided to embark on a path of hormone replacement therapy involving a testosterone pellet implant.

This is transparency. This is why I recommend reading *Feel Sexy Again*. We need people like Erica who are honest and open about the process of surviving and thriving in this selfie society.

Her Four L's (Love, Live, Lift, Leap) will give you the toolkit to continue this journey beyond the short-term transformations. Continuing the journey, continuing to feel sexy (again), is the destination.

Enjoy. Laugh. Share. Erica's insights and wit will keep you reading. Then, take action.

And…Feel Sexy Again.

— **Dan John**, Strength Coach, Author, Professor

Introduction

It all started with a pink wig. Yep. Funny how one little accessory can change the course of one's life – mine, in particular. I don't remember if I bought it for my preschooler's school auction, or perhaps this was pre-kids, not pre-K. What I do know is that I got it in the Gaslamp District in San Diego, California, and that I was so excited to wear it.

Hmm, if my kids weren't born yet, and I most likely didn't buy it for a Halloween costume, what was my desire in purchasing this cute little pink pageboy wig?

Whatever my original idea might have been, this item became a hallmark of what would become my alter ego, Cherry Luminary. Cherry is my diva name, blessed by my beloved friend Portia Diane. (Yes, this is his diva name. He has many others, but this is my favorite.)

Cherry was born at a time when I was searching –

searching to find my true self, my passion, my purpose. She gave me a sense of freedom. She freed me of my own self-judgment and criticism. She allowed me to express my shadow, the dark parts of my being that I hid away. She allowed this expression so that I could step into my wholeness and accept myself in my entirety. I am the light and the dark.

But she was dismissed for awhile. And she was ignored for a long time until she demanded to be seen. She persisted until she won. She will never be ignored again. She helped me discover my story and find my way in the world. Because Cherry is not separate from me. She is me.

She helped me feel comfortable in my skin.

She helped me reclaim the desires I felt were not deserved.

She allowed me to feel sexy again.

Chapter 1:

Ah, the Glory Days

Feeling seen. Feeling desired. Feeling loved. When these are present, we feel whole, connected, and alive. It's that time in your life when you remember what it felt like to feel wanted and powerful. You loved your life and felt like you could take on the world. Nothing could stop you. You worked hard to obtain the education and knowledge for that great career. You fell in love and got married to that amazing guy who adored and worshipped you. You had kids and created a safe and loving life for them. You gave them everything. You wanted your kids to have a secure and happy childhood. You wanted to give them what you didn't have growing up. You were determined to give this to them. You worked hard to provide for your family. And you were content with that. You knew you gave them the best of what you could give. And you created this beautiful life for you and your family. If you look back, you kind of got everything you wanted, everything you fought so hard to have. For a good while, things were pretty perfect.

And then, as it always happens, there came a time when things changed. Our lives do that, don't they? You can't really pinpoint the specific time; it just sneaks up on you when you're not prepared. You can never be prepared when your marriage shows signs of difficulty and you become worried for the future of your relationship. You weren't prepared for when your work demands pushed the boundaries into your personal and family lives and took you away from the ones you loved. You weren't prepared for all the ways your kids needed way more attention, care, and supervision. You weren't prepared for the financial insecurities and trying to make ends meet. You weren't prepared for when you realized you lost yourself in all of the living that happened, and now you don't have a clue on how to find yourself again.

This list is endless, and you weren't prepared for any of it.

It becomes easy to go through life not paying much attention to what happens around you. You get complacent. You get into a groove and stuck in a rut. It takes you more and more away from who you thought you were and what you desired in life. And the more you get away from yourself, the more you feel like you don't have power. And the more you don't feel like you have power, the more you feel lost. Feeling lost is a scary place to be. It makes you question yourself and often your purpose.

On rare occasions, those small windows of recognition surface. You may find yourself saying, "How in the world did I end up here?" "How did I let things get to this point?" For instance, you think about your relationship and how it's changed so much – how he's changed so much, or so it seems. Your level of intimacy and passion have waned or may be closer to nonexistent. Neither you nor your husband seems to really even like one another very much. "How did we allow our relationship to veer so far off course?" Who do you blame? Whose "fault" is it, right? Can you get back on track? Do you even want to get back on track? Sometimes just thinking about the work it takes to sustain any semblance of this relationship makes you want to say, "Just forget it." Boy, do I get that.

And in the course of all of this, there's always something else, right? Just as you think you can squeeze in a bit of time for yourself, there's always something more important that seems to come up – kids, husband, work, school, parents, bills. How did you disappear? When did your priorities change? Squeezing in "me time" often seems like more work. It's a chore. And it's not fair. You want to know how this all happened. How were you not able to see this coming and stop it in its tracks? And, if you'd seen it coming, would you have made different decisions? Hindsight – of course, of course.

And, truth be told, you just want to get yourself back – the you who was confident, bold, sassy, and even a tad bit naughty. Yes, admittedly, yes. Back then, you had a clear sense of who you were and who you wished to be. Back then, you felt good in your skin and loved to find pleasure in life. You needed this to fill your soul. And you devoted time to make this a reality for yourself. You made yourself a priority until the rest of life happened and tamped your own desires because you were needed. Because, like everything else that happens in life, we start taking care of others and put their needs before our own. It often is the nature of life.

Yes, you still love being a mom and a wife (most days). Yes, you still love being a good leader and co-worker, a school volunteer, and an active member in your community; all of these things are important and necessary. And you're not going to stop doing these important and necessary tasks that you have set up as part of your identity. You're not going to run off and leave your family, husband, and community to join Cirque du Soleil anytime soon (ah, but if only).

If only you could find a way to get back to finding balance in your life. If only you could find a way to figure out where you stand in your relationship and take action on it. If only you could recapture the feelings of being wanted, desired, and loved. If only you could rediscover that confidence you once had and find that sexy self who is waiting to emerge.

I want to tell you that I know what it's like to not feel seen. I know what it's like to not feel desired. I know what it's like to not feel sexy or confident in a struggling marriage.

How do I know this? Because I have been there, too.

Chapter 2:

Girls Just Wanna

Growing up, I wanted to be pretty – not cute, but pretty. Cute girls didn't get noticed. Cute girls didn't get the hot guys. Cute girls didn't really have all the fun. (And to be clear, I wasn't even sure what kind of fun I thought I was missing out on. All I knew is that I wasn't having the kind of fun I believed the pretty girls experienced.) Why did I think this was true? Because I was the cute girl. And that was always my experience. I was the smart girl, the athletic girl, the nice girl all through school. I received awards and accolades in support of these characteristics.

While I enjoyed these parts of me, inside I just wanted to shine. I wanted to be adored, worshipped for my beauty. Man, it's embarrassing to think how badly I wanted this. It sounds like I watched way too many Disney movies back in the day. But as a young girl, and a young woman, I saw time and time again how being pretty and being beautiful had its advantages over intelligence, wit, kindness, and grace.

Unfortunately, I looked for every opportunity to see what I saw through this particular lens. I saw what I did because that's what I wanted to see. It was something I felt I could never have. I thought that everything I didn't get or everything that went wrong had to do with me not being pretty enough. Again, it was super foolish thinking, but that was my thought.

I'd always worked hard in school and got great grades. My teachers adored me. I was a Junior Olympic gymnast. I was an incredible dancer. I was funny and intelligent, generous and kind. That should've been enough. But it never is, is it? Throughout my high school years, I longed to be that girl who "had it all": the looks, the boys, the confidence. What I didn't know was that I had so much more than I could comprehend at that time, and these girls who I yearned to be like were also suffering. They tried to be someone else. They tried to be the version of how others saw them. They tried to measure up to who they believed they needed to be. They were insecure, scared, and longing. Just like me. In the end, we all tried to be someone else and not the gorgeous, authentic creatures we were (and are).

Ah, authenticity. My eyes finally opened when I went away to college. This really was a gamechanger for me. I made friends with a couple of gorgeous girls in the dorms. They were stunning beauties. At first, the old insecurities crept in: "I'm not good enough," "I'm not worthy." But, a true revelation occurred. On the outside, they had it all, everything I'd always wanted growing up; internally, though, they were wrecks – each one of them. Soon, they could no longer hide the pressures they placed on themselves. They were truly out of integrity, and it did a number on each one of them in some form or another. That was what I needed to change the way in which I perceived myself. I didn't have to measure up to those girls who I deemed as beautiful. I just had to be me.

I was confident. I didn't need to be the prettiest girl in the room. The hottest girl in the room was the one who held herself with grace. She was the one who could carry on a witty conversation. She was the one who didn't overdo her look and was comfortable in her clothing and in her skin. I realized that being sexy does not equal striking beauty; sexy means confidence and being genuine in how you express yourself. That helped me throughout my college years and earlier adult years.

Later on, however, a different issue came to pass. As confident and secure as I became in my younger adult years, once I entered married life with kids, I became the woman who became the pleaser and lost her sense of identity through being a wife and mother.

I think for many women growing up – with the thought of marriage, kids, and that whole package – it seems almost natural to be selfless and to give oneself over to caring for her husband and children. I felt I was quite liberal growing up and didn't necessarily adhere to the prescribed notion of the man and woman – he the provider, she the stay at home mom. Ironically, though, that is how my first marriage played out, for the most part. I saw my mom struggle in a marriage in which financial struggles were a constant. She worked full time to make ends meet while my dad chased the "big deals" in real estate (never caught one) and was always gone. I didn't want this kind of life for me.

I married a man I knew – I guess subconsciously – would be a good provider and good father: stable, solid, reliable. And he was. He was also absent often and someone who really wasn't my ideal mate for life.

Please place the oxygen mask on yourself first before assisting others. Um, duh, right? If we need to do this in an actual airplane emergency, we cannot be good for anyone else if we are running out of air, so of course we are going to take care of ourselves first. Then why do we go around helping everyone else with their masks while we run around with depleted oxygen, acting like we are full and satiated but actually gasping for air and dying?

Why do we insist on taking care of others while neglecting our basic needs? Seriously?

We fear we will stop being liked or loved and they will leave. Newsflash: people judge us no matter what. Those who truly love us will stay with us. What's going on may be difficult, but they usually adjust. Communication is important, here, of course.

I want to feel needed. I want to be seen as a tireless nurturer. It is my purpose. I am proud of how much I give. Who am I if I start to put myself first? That will change every relationship I have, and that would be scary. People will certainly leave me, call me selfish, a bad mom, a bad wife, a bad coworker.

In 2017, I experienced every major life transition, save divorce, within a span of six months. And, to be honest, divorce was on my mind more than I want to admit. My family and I downsized from a large home to a home half its size. I'd been traveling out of state to help care for my father who had cancer and ended up dying several months later. My teen daughter was out of control and acting out in unhealthy ways, so I made the decision to send her out of state to live with her father, my ex-husband. My current husband struggled with finding a job, and our financial situation was bleak. My son, who has an autoimmune disease that affects his colon, was admitted to the hospital due to rapid weight loss and symptoms that still have no known cause.

To say this took a toll on me is a gross understatement. This affected every aspect of my health: mental, emotional, physical, spiritual. And yet, through all of it, I continued to try to be all things to all people without taking care of my own needs. I hadn't made myself a priority before this chaos; I continued to put everyone before myself during and even after all of this.

Then, I started having thoughts about running away

and leaving everyone behind. I fantasized about leaving my family, and I knew it was not healthy. I also allowed my normal healthy behaviors to slip through the cracks. I am, normally, a very health conscious person. During this time, I stopped eating well and exercising on a regular basis. I overdrank to soothe my anxious feelings. I cried constantly. I snapped at everyone for the littlest annoyances. I couldn't focus on seemingly simple tasks. I felt constantly distracted and foggy. I had little interest in being intimate or having sex with my husband. I didn't care to be around him or, frankly, almost anyone. I was sick and tired of everything. I felt depressed, hopeless and lost. Did I need to be on medication? Quite later on, I went to the doctor and got blood work done to discover that, as a perimenopausal woman with these symptoms, I had a testosterone level of near zero. I made one of the best decisions of my life, for me, and began taking testosterone pellet implants that changed my world for the better – better than better, actually.

I lay on my bathroom floor one afternoon, sobbing uncontrollably. I felt so helpless, so alone, so sorry for myself and something within me shouted, "Stop it. I am so sick of being so sick and tired." And somewhere inside, this observer – someone other than my ego – told me that it was time to quit this nonsense and start living my life. Quit this nonsense and find myself again.

And in that instance, I knew I had to pick myself off that floor and begin anew. I had to stop allowing circumstances to dictate my life. I had to let go of all the control I thought I had over everything that was totally out of my control and focus on the control that I had: I could change my thought. I didn't have to think this way. I could choose another way of thinking. And when I realized that by choosing how I thought, I could affect how I felt. I recognized I could make a choice on how I wanted to feel. How I felt would determine what actions I would take next, which would then have a certain outcome. I could determine what outcome I wanted to achieve.

Intellectually, I knew that this was the way to live. I knew this. For years, I'd studied this type of mindset work. This is the foundation upon which I coach my clients. But being bombarded with one stressor after another took all logic and reason out of the picture. I worked from a reactive survival mentality. I couldn't see anything else. I allowed myself to get so wrapped up in the dark, bleak, miserable feelings of self-pity. The veil was finally lifted that day when I saw myself in this pathetic situation. Something snapped inside of me.

I had been choosing to suffer, and I was over it. I didn't want to be this weak, helpless creature. That wasn't me. The parts of me who are the champion, the optimist, the fighter, the savior, the nurturer, the caregiver – they picked me up off the floor and got me to see me for who I really was and who I was determined to be.

I looked at myself in this moment and truly realized that I had all the power to change how I thought, which led to how I felt, which determined how I decided to act, and what outcome I wanted as a result. At this point, I knew I had to make changes: I had to stop feeling sorry for myself and thinking I could change anyone or anything else, and I had to live the life I knew I was capable of. I knew that if I wanted to continue on in my life, I had to do things differently, and I had to start right then and there.

I couldn't change my circumstances; I could change how I dealt with them. I had to let go of wanting to control everything in my life that didn't go according to my "plan." And that's exactly what I did.

Chapter 3:

The Sexy Again Method

Do you want to reconnect with the sexy person you used to be? Do you crave that feeling of being sexy again? As you can tell by my story, I know how to get you back on track to finding your spark again. I have guided dozens of women along this same journey with a process I developed called the Sexy Again Method. This is an eight-step process that will result in you feeling sexy again and reclaiming your sexual confidence.

In Step 1, I will guide you to assess how you got here at this point in life and how to own your story.

With Step 2, I will help you identify your empowered definitions of sexy, dispel myths, and invite the possibilities of how sexy fits into your life now. In Step 3, I will teach you how you can access these feelings and tap into a sexy-feeling state that is natural and desirable. For Step 4, I will support you to recognize your values, beliefs and goals so that you may become crystal clear on what drives and motivates you in your life. In Step 5, I will invite you to acknowledge and transform old patterns that may be holding you back from knowing you deserve to feel sexy. With Step 6, I will pave the way for understanding your power and ability to change your mindset to get the results you want. You will solidify your desire to express your full potential so you can feel sexy and revitalized in Step 7. And in the final step, Step 8, I will discuss supportive methods and strategies to keep your sexy alive for good.

As you look at these steps, it may feel a bit overwhelming. Hang in there with me. Let me tell you how this process changed my client's life and her marriage.

Debbie became a client of mine during my time as a certified life and wellness coach for a weight loss and fitness retreat. She wanted to lose weight, decrease major work stress, and deal with unresolved grief of an on-again-off-again marriage. We worked with these issues, and developed strategies and plans to support her desired goals. We built a strong co-creative relationship in that time. Along the way, she revealed that she felt she completely lost her sense of self and struggled to find the Debbie who was sassy, soulful, and lustful. She longed to find what pleased her again. She no longer knew how to tap into that part of herself. She was desperate to "reclaim her sexy" and said she'd do anything to solve this problem. When she graduated from the retreat, she hired me to work together in private practice so we could continue the work we started. This process took a solid shape as we moved through this cocreation. As Debbie worked through these steps, her life shifted in ways that she couldn't even imagine. She lost the weight that seemed so challenging to lose; her stress level at work was almost negligible and her on-again-off-again marriage was on – and on strong. And the best part of all: she reclaimed that sexy self she was so desperate to find. She found herself and she's never letting go.

Think of this as a simple step-by-step guide that you can go through cover to cover. I suggest reading it through once and letting it all soak in. I ask questions throughout the book that you may want to answer in the moment or come back to at a later time to reflect upon further. Use a journal or just simply ponder these questions and determine how you wish to use these to get that spark going again.

Chapter 4:

How Did I Get Here?

Sharing stories is one of the most poignant ways in which we can connect with one another. It allows us to feel seen and heard. And if someone's story isn't similar to our own, being able to empathize and really put oneself in the other's shoes goes a long way. My client, Rachel, told a story that, I know, resonates with so many women. And, like with many of my clients, I can find myself in her story.

She couldn't recall exactly when she lost her sense of self. Was it during pregnancy or after having her twins? Sure, she went through that period when breast-feeding and cleaning up after the little poop factories felt like her sole occupation. Her body belonged to "my beautiful little leeches" (so fondly nicknamed). She was designed to nurture and feed her little loves. And for a good while, it didn't bother her. Motherhood was what she'd dreamed of after all, and it was all-consuming. This is what she signed up for.

Until one day, she noticed herself in the mirror. "What the heck is happening to my body?" Her body had changed in ways she could never, ever fathom. She couldn't even recognize her breasts as hers (and most definitely not her husband's; they were strictly "hands off"), let alone the rest of her. "No one really tells you the honest truth about that. Sure, you hear things but don't think it's really going to happen to you. One day you're feeling hot and enjoying sexy time with the hubby, and the next you've got these little human piranhas at your breasts twenty-four-seven and feeling anything but hot and sexy." And what often happens? That not-so-hot feeling turns into days, weeks, years. Time passes and pretty soon you can barely remember you had any spark at all.

Rachel loved her body at one time. She loved the

feelings of excitement and anticipation and having control over her pleasure. Oh, she loved feeling pleasure, of being pleasured. How she missed this. And yet, she felt as if it were a silly dream. It was going to take a lot of time and effort to get back to how she used to feel and look. She had more important things to be concerned about. She recognized that her kids were older now and she should take better care of herself, but added that they always needed something. When she finally had the time, she'd eventually get around to carving out some time for herself.

Does Rachel's story sound at all familiar?

Did you disconnect from yourself somewhere along the way? Maybe it wasn't kids or marriage. Maybe it was a demanding job or career. Or it was school or family or something else. Maybe it was too much of something or just not enough of something else. Whatever caused this rift between you and the version of you that you long for, I am here to tell you that hope does exist.

It starts with redefining who you are now and where you want to be. This may come as a surprise, but your identity constantly changes whether you want it to or not. New ideas, experiences, and situations come left and right. They shape you as they happen. You can't *not* change. But problems arise because you want to stay the same. You need to stay the same. If you change, in any way, then who are you? You may also no longer feel safe when you step outside your comfort zone.

Your brain relies on this sense of comfort and knowing because a millennia ago, it was a matter of life and death. Walk the path. Don't get eaten by a predator. Repeat the same path. Day in, day out. Stay alive. Try an unknown route that one time? Higher chance of becoming lunch. (It happened to the neighbor just yesterday!) Doing "the usual" and staying in your comfort zone is a survival mechanism, but here's the thing: that threat of being eaten by a saber-toothed tiger no longer exists. Your primitive brain still has the collective memory of this occurring; therefore, it wants to protect you. It wants you to stay small and safe. When you do something that is against your default, against the known survival protocol, not only will your brain alert you to impending danger, but your body will, too. Your fight-or-flight system goes into action. Even when you know that going out of your norm is for the better, your system sends you warning signals: your heart races, you may sweat, you may feel sick to your stomach, you may shake or become clumsy, experience myriad other physical and physiological symptoms. And, your brain is doing the second-guessing game, "No, no. Now is that really a good idea? You could get hurt. You could change. Where will that leave you?"

Has this ever happened to you, in one form or another, when you decided to make a change?

Let me go back to Rachel's story. She came to me at a time when her story of not feeling hot and sexy anymore because she had kids and too many responsibilities was her comfort zone. It was the story she told herself. And she lived this story. She told the story and the story became her. She could no longer separate herself from the story.

As we delved into this issue in our coaching sessions, it became apparent that she, indeed, wanted to change this about herself. She craved feeling sexy and desirable again. It petrified her to look at her life from this perspective because she knew she'd have to make a change. And, the thought of changing rocked her self-identity. Who would she be if she chose to feel differently about herself? What actions would she take based on this new information? How would her husband, family, friends think of this version of her?

Well, as we worked with the Sexy Again Method,

she willingly stepped outside of the norm, moving forward one small step at a time. As we addressed her fears and tackled them together, something came into focus for her. She admitted that, strangely, her biggest fear was how her husband would respond to her. She was worried that he would leave her. She further worried that he wouldn't think of her as the caretaker of the family but as selfish and greedy.

Working out her courage to talk to her husband about this, she came back to me after a couple of weeks. She had found a way to speak to him about her needs, and he couldn't have reacted more opposite than what she'd expected. He was absolutely elated and confessed he dreamed of this: that his wife felt good about herself again, felt sexy again. Their love life skyrocketed. This seemed to create a domino effect in every realm of their lives.

Rachel worked tremendously hard to get to this point. She was ready to begin the process. She hadn't been ready for a long time. She carried so much guilt. She had it in droves. She wondered who she really was if she wasn't the dutiful wife, perfect mother, model employee.

Do you ever experience this feeling? This, "I feel

guilty because I want to feel like I want to be me again: not a mom, not a wife, not a dedicated employee ready to do more, be more, give more" feeling?

Do you show your worthiness in this way? The more you give, the more you are seen as good enough. You want to be seen as worthy, good, capable, and enough, but when did this become something that was outward? Why did the judgment of others or someone's approval mean more than your own internal satisfaction? When did this happen? Perhaps it's been going on for a lot longer than you wish to admit. Why now? Why balk at that system and get back to what you want: see to your needs and desires? Because that is exactly why: you lost your sense of self. You are so wrapped up being all to everyone else. And it is exhausting. And you feel guilty that you're not going to be enough for your family, husband, work, friends.

You don't think of stress as being a bad thing. But lately, you get the sense that it's affecting your life in negative ways.

Hey, you are where you are now. It's okay. You go through these periods in life where it takes you on these weird, circuitous, out-of-the-way paths. You may get lost for a while; it happens. You can find a way back. Back to home, back to center, back to you.

You can get so caught up in everyone else's lives, getting serious cases of comparisonitis and FOMO (fear of missing out). It keeps you from living your own life, plain and simple.

Were you taught to put others first? Were you nice, helpful, generous? This was love. If your mother sacrificed on your behalf, this was love. You sacrifice your own needs for the needs/wants of your family. This is the script that is laid down in your hardwiring – thick and implacable. Denying your own personal needs becomes habitual. "My needs/wants aren't as important as others. Others are more worthy. They need nurturing. I will show them they are loved, and they will love me in return."

Do you remember a time in your life when you just had it all going on? You felt in your prime, as if everything felt like the world was on your side? You had this sense that you could rule the world. You felt comfortable in your skin, you felt sexually "on," you were on fire. That sense of sexiness was embodied within you. You knew you were sexy, and not just that external sense of sexiness and attractiveness; you felt, internally, that sense of pleasure. Pure pleasure from all angles. Feeling authentic and not apologizing for expressing who you were. Not to say you didn't have hang ups about your body – we all do. But it was okay. That sense of: "I know what turns me on. And I'm going to take in the experiences and use them to the fullest."

At what point did all of that stop? When did you begin to allow that to slip away, allow it to not be so important in your life?

It's different for everyone; however, I think so often when we become wives and mothers, busy with career and work, dealing with life stresses can take over and we take a back seat in our own lives.

How often do you put everyone else's needs above all else? How often when you just want to say no do you say yes to others for fear of judgment, being seen as selfish, or being disliked or unloved if you say no? So many of us grew up with seeing parents, especially moms, sacrificing themselves for the betterment of the family. You grow up with these scripts that write themselves on your brains and these develop into the stories you tell yourselves, the stories that you live out.

It's your limiting beliefs and these old stories that get replayed over and over and over again.

As you replay these old tapes in your head, they

become your narrative. The thought of doing something different, something that is outside your "norm," seems nearly impossible, even if it's something you desire.

What it comes down to is this: you have to be able to acknowledge where you are right now and how you got to this point in life. This isn't easy. This isn't pleasant. This is hard work. Lessons need to be learned if you want to live in a way that is authentic. Being raw and vulnerable and showing your insecurities, your imperfections is a scary place to be. Vulnerability is crucial to connection. You have to risk in order to truly connect with others. Deep down, you want to be seen. You want to be seen and know you matter in this world.

Here's the deal: You get what you focus on, not want you want. Start putting your energy toward what you actually want versus what you don't want, what's not going right in your life. When you shift your energy toward what you truly want and desire, that changes everything. The power is in the focus. And you get to choose what that is. So, how do you want to feel? Do you want to get your "you" back? Do you want your sexy back? (Cue JT!) Well, let's figure out what your idea of sexy is and how it fits in your life.

Chapter 5:

What Is Sexy, Anyway?

Merriam-Webster (11th ed.) defines "sexy" as:
1. sexually suggestive or stimulating;
2. generally attractive or interesting.

Sexy synonyms and related words, according to *Merriam-Webster*, are:
1. sexually attractive: bodacious. desirable, dishy, hot, luscious, toothsome, foxy, nubile, hunky, alluring, seductive, sultry, vampish
2. of, relating to, exciting, or expressing sexual

> attraction or desire: amorous, aphrodisiac, erogenous, erotic, steamy, carnal, fleshy, sensual, sensuous, bawdy, lascivious, lewd, lustful, obscene, prurient, racy, spicy, suggestive, titillating, dirty, filthy, foul, indecent, nasty, pornographic, ribald, smutty, vulgar, perversive

Which ones resonate with you? Which ones make you feel totally uncomfortable? Which ones make you feel uncomfortable because you actually want to be a bit more like it and it feels, well, dirty? And filthy and nasty, but also erotic, desirable, and maybe a little bit steamy?

No one feels these feelings all of the time. Okay, a few outliers exist, maybe. But just like every feeling, you can feel a little more or a little less depending on the day or the hour. The question herein lies: How do you want to feel? Under which circumstances would it be appropriate to feel sultry? Lustful? Vulgar? And when? Can you imagine these feelings with only your spouse? Alone? How about with a group of friends or coworkers? And, if you feel sexy, does that mean you are looking to have sex? Or will you think others are thinking you want to have sex?

Navigating all of these thoughts can be slippery. "What are my expectations? What are the expectations of others? Can't I just feel sexy without having to think about sex at all? Can't I just express feeling comfortable in my body without the expectation of having sex?" The answer to those questions is, yes, definitely.

Today, when being hot and sexy seems to be the standard in getting noticed, getting liked, and getting laid, a great pressure exists to try measure up. It may feel as if you're losing the battle and the war.

We live in the age of selfies and sexting. Being hot gives girls and boys social currency and significance. It's the ultimate high school popularity contest in virtual form. And, it's never ending. Social media use certainly affects our psychological well-being. It does have its positive benefits, most certainly. However, it's also led to an increase of depression, anxiety, loneliness, and social isolation.

If you are even close to being in your forties, well, think about yourself when you were a teen or young adult. Imagine back then having full access to your wildest fantasies in the palm of your hand. (Today, you may be making up for lost time, but I digress.) I was born in 1970. I was a teen in the eighties. MTV, Atari, VHS – those were our social media. And if we wanted to talk to someone, especially if it was someone we liked, we'd take the receiver off the wall and stretch the phone cord so it could reach the other room, or the closet, if we were lucky. That was about the most privacy we were afforded. And, now? Private conversations happen in plain sight, and not a single word is spoken. Kids watch porn while their parents sit across the table.

Porn culture. I do not believe porn is bad. It most certainly has its place. Yes, if you must know, I watch it once in a while. And, yes, I am a woman. The grave concern is that children have access to this material at such a young age. They're still in the beginning stages of developing their own sexual identities and may often form unhealthy ideas and boundaries about sex. Porn sex isn't real sex. It's about performance. It's about making money. It's to shock and awe. Women and men, on the whole, don't look like this, nor are their body parts representative of the rest of society. But as kids and teens become more desensitized to the images and scenarios they see on the screen, it affects how they internalize their own beliefs about sex and relationships and not in the healthiest ways. Not only does it create highly unrealistic expectations of women and intimacy, but it has also led to an unsettling increase in erectile dysfunction for men in their teens and twenties. These days, the average age for first viewing porn is eleven years old. This comes from a report that draws on more than fifty global studies, involving more than fifty thousand people. "Pornography Consumption and Satisfaction: A Meta-Analysis" concludes that porn shapes our real-world sexual expectations, often with disappointment and frustration.

In her book, *Pornland*, Gail Dines explores how porn hijacked our sexuality, and specifically, young men's sexuality. Gonzo porn – the hard-core type that depicts body-punishing and demeans and dehumanizes women – is what seems to be littered all over the internet. In pre-internet days, mainly soft-core porn existed. It was not easily accessible; usually it was stolen from an older man in the household and was "used" sporadically. Today, having an all-access pass to these extreme images and situations has dramatically changed the sexual landscape for those in the process of exploring and establishing their sexual identities.

What about selfies and such? How does this phenomenon measure up? Is this also damaging the psyche of our youth today?

My daughter is seventeen years old. She and her friends constantly take selfies in various states of undress and provocative poses. It's absolutely maddening. I feel she's objectifying herself. I feel she's putting herself at risk. As a parent of teens (and a fiery, independent, strong-willed teen daughter, in particular) in this day and age, I feel a chronic state of panic, worry, frustration, and protection. I don't want her to expose herself to the world of creeps and perverts. They are looking. I tell her this. She doesn't care. She, like so many other girls of her generation, says it's about empowerment and control over her body. I've read countless articles and stories and listened to frustrated parents, caregivers and educators.

I am not alone in my feelings. I think back to when I was her age. I didn't have access to any of what she does today. I wonder how I would've behaved if given this technology. Who knows? Here's the thing: It's a natural progression of transitioning from girls to teens to young women to adulthood. Sexual identity is part of that exploration.

It's a fine line. I want to protect her. I want her to be safe. I want her to be smart. She's navigating this new, unchartered territory of sexuality in the way in which feels natural to her. This seems to be the case for many other young women. We elders can say that their self-objectification is doing irreparable damage to their future. Look around: this self-exposure certainly seems to be their way of getting attention; it also seems to be a way of chronicling their lives, like a visual diary. It's a format and platform to allow you and others to share who you are and document your existence.

As girls and young women feel the pressure to be perfect, hot, sexy, and likable to get noticed, women of all ages also feel this pressure. It's not just advertisements selling products to buy; it's a culture of selling ourselves every single day. We sell ourselves to get the external validation from others.

Youth is king. You can take a selfie with all the filters to smooth, tan, or even lighten your skin; remove the wrinkles, adjust your facial "imperfections" so that you look years younger. This is what social media is telling you to do in order to look hotter and more desirable. And, if you do this, it means that you'll get asked out or offered the job or get that promotion, right? It may not be you in your most authentic self. It's the version of yourself you think others will see as authentic. And, after all, isn't that what really matters? We've become so conditioned to this way of life. I'm not saying this is a good thing, but it has become part of our society's new normal. It's easy to get jaded and get on our high horses, but I can say that I've been guilty of trying to show my "best self," which included dozens of tries at one picture that wasn't quite right, just to get the perfect "authentic" shot. Yes, I'm guilty. I drank the Kool-Aid.

But, at the same time, I am also understanding how the role of this way of communication and being seen is subjected to the external. It leaves little room to rely on our internal resources of what it means to be lovable, good enough, and accepted in today's society.

It's up to you to become brave and empowered, to stand up and say this is not the be-all, end-all of how you define yourself. You don't have to follow these scripts. You don't have to be part of the system that tells you that you are not worthy enough or lovable enough if you don't take part in what they tell you you should do. Forget that!

We have lost much of the ability to rely on our internal sense of self and what that truly means to us. If we strip away all the garbage, the superficiality, the fakeness, and the inauthentic ways of showing up in the world – both for ourselves and for others – what would have to come from within to acknowledge that we are acceptable, lovable, worthy, and capable? We'd have to use our own internal strengths to tap into that power that resides within us.

It's an uphill battle, to be sure. What does this mean for us? Do we give in to it all and continue the quest of the external: seeking approval of others, which will, by extension, allow us to approve of ourselves (as so many believe to be the case)?

Can you imagine feeling the love and acceptance and self-worth and desire coming from an internal source, coming from you? Imagine all the opportunities that can be available to you if you decide how you want to feel – independent of anyone and anything else. Man, what would that really feel like? Scary? Impossible? Expansive? Limitless? Possible? Oh, it's absolutely possible, yes. How, you may ask?

Let me first speak to what countless women have deemed "sexy" for themselves (keep in mind that this is a partial list that just scratches the surface):

- Feeling good in my body, in my skin
- Accepting me for all of me: flaws and all
- Appreciating how my body moves, how it

- supports me, how it carries me through life
- Knowing that I am intelligent and strong and secure
- Tapping into the senses and the sensual pleasures of life: taste, sound, scent, movement, touch, sight; tuning into every part of my being
- Being able to give and receive pleasure, both sexual and nonsexual, self-satisfaction
- True lack of self-consciousness
- Spark of sureness
- Poised, not arrogant
- Truth – being unequivocally myself
- Confidence

Every single one of these speaks about confidence. Time and time again, confidence seems to be the determining factor in how one moves about in the world. We can all have varying degrees of confidence. It waivers. We aren't "all or nothing" on this front. We have dark, dreary days when our confidence is near zero. We have other days when we are on cloud nine, top of the world, and our confidence level is sky high.

Stop for a moment and think about feeling confident. How does your body actually feel? Think from a somatic or kinesthetic perspective: scan your body. What do you notice? What's happening with your neck, shoulders, back, face, hands, chest, hips, stomach, legs, feet? As you mindfully check in with these parts of your body, pay attention to how they feel. Open? Closed? Tight? Relaxed? Receptive? Restrictive? How about your energy level? What form of energy are you putting out when you are in a confident frame of mind? What energy do you attract? We get what we focus on, right? The power is in the focus. If you focus on the confident energy that lies within, what are the possible outcomes resulting from that confidence?

I can think of a powerful example of how this may be attained: power posing. In an October 2012 TED talk, social psychologist, Amy Cuddy, presented that "your body language shapes who you are." Having a powerful presence puts you into a more powerful mindset. How you hold your body can have an impact on your mind.

Don't believe me? Try it. You can either sit or stand for this. Start with the low-power pose. Your chest is hunched in slightly, leaning inward, and your legs are crossed if you are sitting. Do this for two minutes. Then, for another two minutes, try on the high-power pose. You have an expansive posture (think Wonder Woman or Superman: chest open, hands on hips, head up, eyes looking straight out to the horizon). Notice any difference?

Have you ever heard the phrase "act as if?" Take it a step further and act until you become it, until you embody how you want to feel.

Your hormones may even be linked to this: there is a correlation of feeling powerful with higher testosterone levels and lower cortisol levels.

The more you practice and master new skills, the more your brain begins to actually rewire neurons. This can allow you to get out of your old default mode, negative thought loops, and create real and lasting change. Your body changes your mind, which changes your behavior, which changes your outcomes.

If you have the ability to change the way you think and feel, then let me ask you: What makes you feel sexy? What makes someone else sexy in your eyes, both men and women, alike? Oftentimes, what you notice about others and what resonates with others is something that lies within yourself. It may be dormant; it may be screaming from the rafters. It exists within. It's about acknowledging the power and choice you hold and making a conscious decision to change.

Think about how you want to feel. Step into the confidence, into the person you wish to be. Can you imagine it? How might you take a single step toward that direction? How might your life be different if you take that step and watch how the momentum takes hold? Hmm, I'm getting hot and steamy just thinking about it.

Chapter 6:

Can I Reignite This Feeling?

You are ready to rekindle this missing piece of yourself, yes? You are ready to embrace that alluring, steamy, luscious creature that resides inside you. You are ready, yet you haven't a clue how to access her.

How can you tap into this energy?

How much of your significance is tied to how others think and feel and act toward you? Can you imagine standing alone in your power, accepting your significance independent of anyone else? Can you imagine not being the "perfect wife," "perfect mother," "perfect daughter," et cetera, and the world not falling apart? Can you imagine being "good enough" and that actually being enough? Whoa, scary thought, right? Maybe also somewhat liberating? Just maybe. What if you are ready to feel this way? How might you start this journey?

Can you think of a time when you felt completely alive and vibrant and authentic? You felt completely you. You were in your element. You were in flow. This flow state is a state in which your body leads. Your body takes over and you are totally immersed in an experience; you are free of worry, judgment, self-consciousness. You simply exist. You are in a moment that is absolutely pure, raw, and euphoric.

I've been a dancer for the majority of my life. It is one of my greatest pleasures. Within the last year, I took a class, called S Factor, that uses feminine, body-led movements. Lower levels start with choreography to introduce a series of movements that, for most, are unnatural. I say they are "unnatural" because most of us don't move this way. It is seductive. It is naughty. It is, perhaps, impolite in everyday society (think twerking but with much more panache and for your own pleasure, not for performance or attracting attention.).

This is uncomfortable and can be quite intimidating.

Many women have a lot of shame, guilt, insecurity, and self-consciousness when it comes to our bodies. This class opens up a lot of fear and anxiety for women when they first attend. It can be scary. We are supposed to connect with our feminine bodies. We are supposed to touch ourselves in a manner that feels good to us – caressing body parts that aren't the norm in our everyday lives. We are led to explore our bodies, establish our body boundaries. We are encouraged to play with touch, movement, and breath. We are to, oh-so-supportively and lovingly, find our pleasure.

This is a process of letting go, acceptance, and self-love. And what happens over time is that the choreography stops at a certain level and the upper levels explore with that body-led movement. We learn a new language, and, as with any new language, over time, we become brain immersed; this new language begins to become embodied within our bodies. We can then allow ourselves to be completely taken over when the music starts. We get out of our heads – being concerned with the right moves and the right choreographic sequences – and we just let go. We let our bodies take over as this new language expresses itself.

I've experienced this more times than I can count

as I've reached the upper levels. I become completely immersed in something other than what my thinking mind can comprehend. My body leads, and I am completely, utterly, in flow. This energy expressed feels like pure magic, resulting in healing, growth and transformation It is the ultimate therapy, indeed.

This class happens once a week, and yet I find myself practicing more and more at home in my limited spare time. There's something profound about giving myself permission to tap into my feminine body, allowing full expression of how my body wants to move, how my body seeks pleasure. Is it erotic? Oh, yeah. Does it help my sex life? Absolutely. But it's not just that; this journey has spilled over into every part of my life. It's given me an entirely new lens in which I see how I occur in the world and how I wish to be. Accepting this feminine part of me has both surprised and elated me. I have a lot of masculine energy, so this ritual of receiving, self-nurturing, being vulnerable, feeling self-love, and not having to give or nurture or love anyone else but me, for a little slice of time, is heavenly. I realized how this has been pretty absent in my life, for most of my life. And I've come to need it now, this raw and beautiful vulnerability. I crave more. And, I'm working on that and finding more opportunities to continue exploring my desire for being in my feminine. Thank you, Sheila Kelley, for opening my eyes to a gorgeous world. (She is the founder of S Factor). If you have any curiosity at all about this practice, check out www.sfactor.com.

This experience also opened my eyes to something quite remarkable: it made me understand that I put the responsibility on my spouse to make me feel loved, worthy, and significant. I've allowed my significance to be tied to how someone else feels about me. If I don't feel loved and supported by my partner, that means that I am not worthy or lovable. And I've done this with every single relationship I've had in my life. Perhaps, dear reader, you can relate to this.

You are in charge of how you feel. No one else is responsible for this. You have the power to feel however you choose; it's not someone else's job to fill that role. You can't blame anyone except yourself. Take a look at your role in how you act/react in the world. Can you take responsibility for your actions/reactions?

What do you crave? Can you tap into that receiving, open, vulnerable energy? Does my S Factor experience excite you? Terrify you? Can you picture yourself experiencing something like this?

If that seems too much for now, let's try another scenario. Close your eyes and take yourself back to a moment in which you felt expansive beyond measure. Take a few cleansing deep breaths. Focus on a time when you felt free and grounded. You felt like, well, you, in the most authentic and self-loving manner imaginable.

It can be an example such as this: Walking on a beach, feeling your toes grabbing the wet sand, smelling and tasting the salty air, the ocean breeze rustling your hair, hearing the crashing of the waves. You feel alive. Whether exhilarated and full of possibility or sentimental and melancholy or any other feeling that comes up, try to fully feel the feelings and experience the senses to their full capacity. Lean in and sit with this sensory experience. What comes up for you?

Now, think about putting yourself in a "state of sexy." What might that entail? What senses need to be awakened and acknowledged? What might you have to elicit in order to tap into this sense for yourself? Can you go there?

Can you see yourself in that sexy state of mind? What may have to be in place in order for you to access this within yourself? Open up to all of your senses. Visualize and think of the details - details, please! The more you can create a full vivid Technicolor picture: sight, sound, smell, taste, touch, the better. Get specific. The more you can embody this new language you are learning, the better. Pay attention. Everything is good information.

Be aware of the little voice inside your head, the tapping on your shoulder, the butterflies that flitter in your gut, the tingly feeling that shoots up your spine. Pay attention to what your inner voice tells you. Don't push her away, bury her, or ignore her. Listen to her. She's trying to tell you something. Be aware. Be open and receptive. Invite her in. Ask her to come and stay awhile. Listen to what she has to say. She is wise. She is knowing. She is love. She is you.

You know, we so often want to show our light – our shiny, perfect, unsullied side – right? We don't want others to see our flaws, our "badness." We often hide this from ourselves.

I see you. I see you for your light and your dark. The dark side holds so much magic and wisdom and truth. And here's the thing: you are the light and the dark. You are whole. You cannot be your true self until you can acknowledge the shadow and, more importantly, accept that it is a part of you. You are not one without the other. When you can embrace this from within and love yourself for your entirety and the well-rounded, exceptional creature you truly are, your power is limitless.

Nothing is sexier than when you see someone who totally embodies self-knowledge, self-acceptance, self-love, and compassion. She is comfortable and confident in who she is. She shines her light so brightly and does not hide in the shadows. She holds the shadow and light simultaneously and revels in the strength she possesses. Now, that is h-o-t, is it not?

What if you're not there yet? I get it. It took me a hot minute to determine if I was ready to enter this world. And once I was there, it could've been a complete disaster or just not a good fit. It just happened to be the best fit for me. You have to find your fit. You have your levels of comfort, and only you know how far you are willing to travel. It takes time. Be gentle with yourself in finding out what that is. Have patience and trust yourself. You may need to get brave and reach out, do some research. That's the wonderful power of the anonymity of the internet. You can research to your heart's content. Ask around. Get curious.

What do you have the desire to try? Start from center and see what your comfort scale looks like when you think of discomfort. Remember this: don't allow your old stories to stop you from your next important risk. Getting in your own way is the only thing that's holding you back. It's what keeps you locked, small, and unwilling to change and grow. Getting out and risking a bit – or a lot – may be just what you need to tap into that spirit and inner voice that is telling you to be, do, act, and become. How will you know anything unless you give it a shot? Yes, it's scary. But will fear – the thing that can be so vast and all-consuming – kill you? What your mind conjures up is so much more frightening than actual reality. Your fear keeps you small and safe, or so it thinks. Those were the days when we had to be worried about every single thing for survival – remember that saber-toothed tiger? Your primitive brain still wants to keep you safe. It's your job to take a look at what it tells you and question the reality, question the reasoning. The unknown is frightening. It's also exactly where you need to journey in order to change and learn and expand. It is the only way.

What if there's no way you want to expose yourself like this? What if this isn't it, but you wish to start something that gets you pointed in the general direction?

Trust the process. Trust that you are able to acknowledge and appreciate the journey and not be laser focused on the outcome. The outcome is important, yes, but you cannot jump from point A to point B. You must put one foot in front of the other and walk toward that goal. It may change. It most likely will change. The path will twist and turn, and roadblocks will present themselves. It is about flow and openness to change. It's about living the process along the way: acting, reacting, growing, changing and expanding. At some point on the journey, you will be able to turn your head, look back and say, "Whoa, look where I came from. I'm so much further along that I imagined. I'm going to keep moving forward." Stop and give yourself the privilege to attention. The destination may or may not change. The path to get there certainly will.

There's this great saying I heard years and years ago, "You can't see the picture when you're inside the frame." It's all about perspective and being open to observing yourself as you move about the world.

As you're opening up about your desires, who do you truly wish to be?

Chapter 7

Who Do I Really Want to Be?

During one of our coaching sessions, my client, Debbie observed, "Being a good mom, a good wife, a good coworker, a good PTA member, I know how important this is. I think most of us do the best we can in this regard. I know I most certainly do. But is it also possible that we can take our roles a bit too far? I feel I've lost myself along the way trying to be good for everyone. I'm sure it happens to all of us. It seems almost necessary for a period of time. But then we seem to keep doing it, doing good for everyone else, except us. We don't think about losing ourselves in this process, until it happens. And, even then, it may take a long while before we can even recognize it, let alone know what to do about it."

New love is a good example. Merging with your lover – what could be more delicious? Remember when you were so intent on spending every waking moment being, literally, attached to one another's bodies? Remember just wanting to get lost in each other? Where did you end and he begin? Ahh, yes. He + I = We. He completes me, and we become we. We is the holy grail for so many, right? Being coupled is often the goal – celebrated and expected in so many cultures. When it's just me, myself and I, often this is seen as not ideal; we are lonely, incomplete. This is changing in our society. Being alone does not equate loneliness.

But how many of us are terrified of being alone? How many of us have been conditioned to be partnered and to meld into that couplehood? Where did we learn this? Often, it is our family of origin, our parents, our caregivers, who give us the first glimpses of these important relationships. Our early experiences shape us, imprint on us the significance of these connections with others. We then take this and try to make sense of how it fits.

For example, I grew up with parents who often

fought. They were verbal, loud, and sometimes volatile. As a young girl, I witnessed these fights. They divorced when I was thirteen years old. This upbringing taught me how to be a peacekeeper. I learned to not rock the boat, and I avoided conflict like the plague. I learned that if I was perfect at school and athletics, if I didn't get in trouble and was a good girl, I could distract them for a while and bring some temporary happiness to our lives. Over the years, I can see how I carried over these survival tactics into my adult relationships. Because I didn't ever want to have my parents' kind of marriage, I created these scripts in order to shield myself from any potential hurt and devastation. I wanted a safe, loving and lasting marriage. I did all I could to be that person I thought I had to be to in order to keep myself safe. I made my voice small. I placated. I was always generous. I avoided conflict at all cost. This is how I behaved in the world. It took me a long time to realize that doing these things still wouldn't protect me from the world, nor would it create the perfect scenario for the perfect relationship. I'd become the person I thought I needed to be, the person I thought I should be. I wasn't the person I truly wanted and desired to be. I hid my own true self for fear that if I showed up as me, that I wasn't worthy of love and safety.

Can you look to when you grew up? Did something leave a lasting impression on you and how you have brought that into your relationships? How did your younger years help shape you into the person you are today? And through these early experiences, what did you come to value in life? What did you grow up believing was true in your life? What are some of your most fundamental beliefs? What are qualities in life that you prioritize above all else?

Years ago, as part of a coach training, one of my many introspective assignments was to research and discover my internal frame of reference: what were my core values in life? How did these values shape the way in which I lived my life? Was I living in or out of alignment with these values? And, if I was living out of alignment, could I recognize this and make efforts to change the way I operated so that I could live more congruently?

I was given a standard values interview of more than one hundred potential values. It asked me to identify my main three core values. I took my time and distilled them down to what most resonated with me. The top three core values that have driven, and still drive, my life today are intimacy (sharing my innermost experiences with others), safety (being safe and secure), and fitness (being physically fit and strong).

These three surprised me at first. They seem like an odd bunching, to say the least. But the more I thought about my past – unraveled certain ideals, goals, beliefs I held and what I wanted in my life in the future – well, these seemed really quite natural.

Intimacy: I desire to connect with others, in the most authentic and genuine way. I need to have people in my life whom I trust, who really know me, and who accept and love me for me.

Safety: I desire to feel safe and nurtured and protected. I desperately need to feel that someone is willing to be there for me in times of need and won't let me down.

Fitness: I desire to be as physically fit and strong as I can for as long as I can. I enjoy the numerous benefits my body offers me when I am able to move about the world with grace and strength and receptivity.

These three values are standards by which I live. These are nonnegotiable. They are ingrained in the deepest part of me. It should be easy, then, to live by these values in my life and all will be accepted, supported, honored, and all will be perpetually well in the world, right? What if you marry someone who doesn't hold those same values? Or maybe he neither cares nor deems them important? And you really want to be with this person, so maybe you put those values aside for a bit. They'll be there, waiting for you, right? Time goes by. They fade. Maybe you even close the door to them as you assimilate and take on your lover's values until one day, you get a nudge, a whisper of those deep yearnings. You are called back to yourself. It's easy to decide to ignore this pull. Choose to listen. The voice will continue. She will become louder and more incessant.

What do you value in life? What is important to you? What matters to you, motivates you? Are you living your life in a manner that supports what you value? Oftentimes, when you feel out of sync and disconnected from yourself, it is related to the incongruency between your actions in life and what you hold as fundamental beliefs.

Having a sense of integrity is behaving in a manner that is consistent with your values. How might you become more congruent, more in touch with your authentic self? And, what about your desire to feel sexy again? What if you don't feel deserving of such feelings? How can you find a way to break this barrier so that you can feel deserving?

Chapter 8:

Why Don't I Feel Like I Deserve to Be Sexy?

Embarrassment. Shame. Guilt. Judgment. Foolishness. These words described my client Jenny's reaction to my question, "What words come to your mind when I tell you that you deserve to feel sexy?" Jenny, who is in her forties, recalled a time as a young teen, just entering her freshman year in high school. She'd just moved to a new state with her family and knew no one. She felt such a strong need to be accepted and liked by her peers: new school, new friends, new life. She also wanted to feel more grown up now that she'd left middle school and was wanting to make an impression that showed others that she was "sophisticated." (Oh, how I remember these days.)

She left the house dressed in a manner that was parent-approved; however, she'd packed a different outfit entirely and changed into it before entering school. She wanted to make the statement that she was no longer a child. Well, this more grown up look got the attention; unfortunately, it was not the type she expected. Kids snickered and whispered during class. She spent that first day alone in the cafeteria being ignored, feeling embarrassed and lonely. From that day, she vowed to herself that she would not stand out and get noticed. She always "dressed normally" so that she could blend in. She never wanted to be the object of any unwanted attention, whatsoever. Eventually, life went on. She made friends and had a decent high school experience. But this one moment still haunts her, even today as a full-fledged adult. She desired to tackle her issues, wanting to let go of how negatively this impacted her.

She and I worked for several months on something called neural conditioning. In a nutshell, neural conditioning is replacing an old story that doesn't serve you with a new story that is ideal and empowering. It works on identifying triggers that you then act on, usually not in a healthy, constructive manner. You want to replace these usual responses with an ideal response or behavior that gives you autonomy and a positive outcome. A personal mantra is set, and the ideal behavior is recognized beforehand. As the emotional trigger comes up, you set your mantra to include a physical focus, a verbal cue and a physiological response, simultaneously.

Any time feelings of shame, embarrassment, or guilt about her body triggered her, Jenny would use her mantra in order to bypass the negative feelings she'd once automatically experienced.

Her mantra was simple: She placed her hands over her heart (physical focus), recited to herself, "I am centered and grounded," (verbal cue) and took three deep cleansing breaths (physiological response). She did this every single time she was emotionally triggered in that way. As she performed her mantra, her ideal response was to focus her attention on a pleasant aspect of her body and smile. This was the task. She performed this dozens of times. It took some effort and work, but slowly, as soon as the negative trigger occurred, she'd start her mantra and find she'd already shifted into smiling and thinking positive images of her body.

This process, "Neural Conditioning to Make Changes That Last," was created by my Mentor, Dave Krueger, MD, founder of MentorPath® (go to www. feelsexyagain.com to download your free copy). It's been a remarkably successful tool for my clients in overcoming old stories and creating new empowered ones.

I am reminded of a profoundly beautiful Zen proverb, "Knowledge is learning something new every day. Wisdom is letting go of something every day."

Can you imagine letting go of what no longer serves in order to make room for the possibilities?

Can you imagine letting go of the fears that prevent you from living a full and true life?

Can you imagine stepping into a mindset that focuses on what you truly desire and going after it?

What is your biggest fear surrounding this issue, going after what you desire? Think about this for a moment. You've lived your life the way you've lived it up to this point. It gets comfortable, right? You live your life according to certain scripts that have been adhered to for, pretty much forever. This hardwiring has been laid down at an early age.

Often, when you think about what else might be available to you in this world, you stop yourself almost instantaneously. "I can't do that. What would my family, husband, children, or friends think? They need me. If I chose to do X, then I may not be there for them. I may abandon them. I am not deserving of the things I truly desire. I need to be selfless and giving and generous to those I love. I need to do what is expected of me. Who am I to be allowed to want what I want? I need to want what my family wants, my friends, my colleagues." Does this ring any bells?

Who are you to live out your dreams? Who are you to have dreams? Your family, your husband, your job – they are your dreams, right? How could you possibly want anything else in life? How could you possibly want for you?

Until you do.

Until you recognize that you want more from your life and then guilt and shame and dread and judgment set in.

You want, but you don't want.

You want, but you feel you shouldn't.

You want, but you don't feel like you're deserving of any of it.

Any of this sound familiar?

Chapter 9:

What Is It Costing Me to Deny My Feelings?

Feeling responsible for the entire world comes at a cost. When I say, "entire world," I am referring to my world: my kids, my husband, my family, my community. They are my entirety. I've structured my life around keeping others happy and safe. I want others, especially those I love, to know that they are loved and supported and seen. It's been my responsibility. It's been my job. And, I've allowed it to consume me. I've been actively working on making sure everyone else was taken care of, and I never really took my own needs or wants into account. I kept myself out of the equation.

I know I'm not alone in this. Can you identify with me, here?

I created this life where I felt responsible for others' happiness and safety. I craved this as a child, so I fought like mad growing up to manifest this in every relationship I forged. I didn't manifest it as much as force it. There's a big difference here.

When I experienced the deluge of major life changes coming at me left and right several years ago, this ripped me from what I believed was truth: that I could keep everyone safe and happy and protected. I couldn't. I can't. Never. Ever. And seriously, I was pretty delusional by thinking I had control over any of it.

You are also mistaken in thinking you have control over your circumstances. News flash: you can't control the weather. You can't control the traffic. You can't control what your husband thinks, does, or doesn't do. You can't control if your kids sneak out of the house, if they get poor grades, or if they smoke pot. You can't control when people get upset with you, leave the relationship, or die. None of it is within your control.

Yet haven't you believed the opposite to be true? You grow up with the knowledge that what you know is the truth. What you know is your truth; it is not someone else's truth. It's what you believe, but it doesn't make it fact. You author your stories and your stories shape who you are. Because you create your stories, you have complete ownership in rewriting the script. Not only do you have ownership in rewriting the script, but you also have the power to write yourself into how you want to continue your story. This is within your power. It also takes a shift in your thinking from what you've always known and always allowed yourself to believe.

Often, the most difficult and necessary choices you make are the ones that seem impossible to achieve. And when you make these choices, you make a decision to change who you are. This isn't normally a conscious thought. However, when you make a decision, it creates a ripple effect. It changes the energy and the landscape. It changes the relationships you have grown to know. You cannot adapt, grow, and change without altering your self-identity. You may crave change but be petrified of the outcome. What does that mean to your life and the lives of the those you love? And, more importantly, who are you if you step into this new identity while leaving the one you know so well behind? What else and who else, might you leave behind as you step into this new version of myself?

I truly believe it took this influx of multiple life changes, of which I had zero control, to bring me to a crossroad. I could succumb to the weight of it all and let it take me under. I could continue living in a manner in which I could blame external forces and not take responsibility for how I wished to live. Or I could be brave – really brave – and release my grip on everything I couldn't control. I'd have to trust the unknown, step into the discomfort and live my life in an entirely new way. I had to become a new version of myself in order to make this happen. I had to risk the potential fallout of not being the same person everyone else knew and relied on. I had to become the person I wished to be so I could live the life I knew I deserved.

I couldn't keep everyone happy or safe or protected from what was happening, though. Being everything to everyone did not work for me. I had to let go of thinking I had so much power over the course and outcome of everyone else's life. I needed to focus on me. I needed to take care of my needs. I needed to treat myself like someone I loved.

A huge hole that desperately needed to be filled was the way in which I saw myself. I'd so longed to feel good again. I wanted to reconnect with my body. I wanted to feel pleasure. I wanted to feel alive.

Honestly, I was just over feeling so sorry for myself. I made a choice to live this way. I couldn't blame anyone or anything else for how I behaved in my world, as much as I wanted to put all my woes onto something else "out there." Isn't it so much easier to place responsibility on someone, something other than us? It's humbling to realize that we have full autonomy and accountability for our actions. It sucks. It's also extremely liberating to acknowledge this, because if we can get out of our own way, we can make room for what is really possible. I mean, it served me well to feel sorry for myself for a time. It's a self-protective mechanism. But at some point, that gets old. As I said, I was totally over myself. I was ready to make changes. It cost me my sanity. It cost me my health. It cost me my relationships. I had to be brave. I had to be vulnerable. I had to ask for help. I had to connect with others in order to feel I wasn't alone, and I had to connect with myself in order to explore what I really wanted for myself.

It was time to find that part of me with whom I

longed to reconnect. It was time to step into a new version of myself and try her on. What did she desire? How did she wish to feel? What excited her and made her feel good? What made her come alive? What did she need to do in order to become the very best version of herself?

What do you desire?
How do you wish to feel?
What excites you? What makes you feel good?
What makes you come alive?
What do you need to do in order to become the
best version of yourself?
What's one small step you can take, right now,
to set you in that direction?
You, my dear, need to know this:
You are worthy beyond measure.
You are capable of anything to which you set
your mind.
You are lovable. No question. No doubt.
Oh, yes you are.
And, this may come as a shock to you:
No one else can make you feel this way.
It starts with you. You must believe this within
yourself. You must take accountability for how

you want to act and how you wish to be treated
in this world. It starts with you. It will always
come back to this.
The great question herein lies:
How do you wish to live this life?
It is absolutely, unequivocally, up to you.

Risk is inherent in pretty much everything you do. You risk when you wake up in the morning. You risk when you get in your car to drive to work. You risk when you fall in love. You risk when you have children. You risk when you quit your job to go out on your own. You risk when you ask for what you truly want. The list is prolific.

Life is about risk. It is also about tremendous reward. Having the courage to stand in the face of fear and move triumphantly past it gives you power and leverage to take control of your life.

What are you willing to risk to live a life that feels genuine and authentic and aligned with what you value in life?

Is it having a difficult conversation with your spouse about what you want from your relationship? Is it telling your adult child it's time to get a job and move out of your basement? Is it telling your boss you have too much on your plate and you will not take on one more task? Is it acknowledging your desires and taking action to make them come to life?

The list goes on and on and on.

Is it possible that you will fail? Yes, this is guaranteed. You will also learn and grow and use this knowledge to try again. You will take a different path. You will continue to try. You will forge ahead. Fail forward. Always. Because this is what allows you to get to the good stuff. It will allow you to succeed. This is what allows you to see the struggles and challenges you've endured and surpassed. Every step you take along your journey leads you to your destination. Your journey will likely twist and turn. You will encounter road blocks and detours. You may veer off for a long while before finding your way back. You may stay on a well-worn path that seemed like the "right path" at the time, only to later decide to venture out and create an altogether new route. Think of Robert Frost's *The Road Not Taken.*

You can always decide to change your mind. You can always decide to take a new path. You can always make a different choice.

When you think back to being "all things to all

people" and putting yourself on the back burner, you can understand that it served a purpose for a time. Your identity was absolutely tied up in this; and you were okay with this then. You are no longer okay with setting yourself to the side. You are ready to live front and center and live on your terms. Can you still take care of your family and be who you need to be for others while still fulfilling your desire to feel alive, sexy, and confident about your life? Yes, without question, yes!

Chapter 10:

I Want to Feel Sexy Again, but Where Do I Start?

Time to breathe, here. Deep breaths. Now, the fun part really begins. It may seem overwhelming on how to move forward. That's totally okay. The beauty is that this time is dedicated to you. You get to decide what this looks like. Does this feel a little selfish? Does the thought of having to pay attention to your needs and desires make you uncomfortable still? Do you worry about how others will judge you for – a crazy thought!–

taking care of yourself? More deep breaths, here. It's time to let go of what you believe others think. It's time to let go of the worry and the undue stress you cause yourself because you allow yourself to feel this way.

Remember that we talked about this. You control your thoughts. You control your emotions. You control your actions. You control the results that follow from those actions. Yes, I know it is hard sometimes to wrap your mind around this concept. We can thank neuroscience and quantum physics for this. It is, again, so much easier to take the onus off ourselves and put someone else in charge. It is time to take responsibility. It is time to be accountable. It is time to acknowledge the wondrous power you possess, if you can be so brave.

Your power may frighten you. You often keep yourself from reaching your full potential because of that fear. Fear of failure? Yes. Fear of success? Absolutely. Your fear of success can be a greater deterrent to moving forward than your fear of failure. Why? When you fear failure, it's often because you assume you are going to fail. You expect it. You go back to what you know. It's back to your comfort zone. But success? If you try something and succeed, you are in unknown territory. Things are different. Things change, as do you. And everything else in your life changes, too. Because you aren't familiar with this new landscape, you're frightened. Your ego wants to keep you predictable and safe. It doesn't want you to go into the dark scary place of unpredictability. You will stay small. If you continue to let your ego rule, you will not succeed. You will not change. You will not grow and transform into your potential and your greatness. You've got to tell your ego to take a hike.

It's time to stop playing small and start jumping into the unknown. It is the only way to become the person you are destined to be.

Let me ask you:

- What do wish to have more of in your life?
- What do you wish to have less of in your life?
- What would you like to eliminate from your life?
- What do you want to enhance in your life?

These questions are important when you take an inventory of what you want in life. Reach out to every corner of your life: Love (romantic/familial), work, spirituality, leisure, health, financial, et cetera.

If it's helpful, get a journal or notebook and jot down your answers. Look at patterns and themes that may occur. No wrong answers exist here. This is something that can give you a starting point in which to gather information and provide possibilities.

Another exercise I love is creating "My Pleasure Principles" list. Think of all your senses. How do you derive pleasure from each of these: sight, sound, taste, smell, touch? Pleasure is open to interpretation. Sexual pleasure? Yes. Nonsexual? You betcha.

Here's one of My Pleasure Principles list from over three years ago. I encourage you to start one for yourself. Again, absolutely no wrong answers, here. Write down everything pleasurable that comes to mind. Let it be fun and free and tap into all the ways in which you find pleasure in your body. Enjoy.

My Pleasure Principles (3/19/16)

- Feeling/sensing how my body moves/reacts – kinesthetic awareness
- Listening/enjoying/getting lost in the moment, esp. with music
- Appreciating my sensual body/reclaiming boundaries of what feels good
- Dancing/feeling rhythm/feminine authentic movement

- Having pleasurable sex/satisfying my partner/ being satisfied in return
- Feeling sexy/strong/capable/desired
- Experiencing soulful connections with others
- Traveling/experiencing new cultures/speaking new languages
- Learning new skills/challenging myself/accomplishing goals
- Working toward new goals
- Loving others/being loved
- Laughing heartily/belly laughing/pure, full, real
- Appreciating nature/hiking/awareness of my surroundings
- Preparing healthy, delicious food/joy of others enjoying my food
- Reading engaging books/reading and writing thoughtful poetry
- Eating/savoring good food and drink
- Smelling scents that elicit positive memories: lavender, lemon verbena, cinnamon, cedar, bergamot, grapefruit
- Enjoying/appreciating art and aesthetic beauty
- Silence/meditation/tranquility/peace
- Breathing deeply and coming back to the

breath

It's probably time I add to this list. But I hope you see the idea. All of these items are great pleasures in my life (sexual and non). Actually, seeing this list is also an important reminder for me to come back to this when I may have an off day or I'm not feeling my most authentic self. Just reminding myself of what gives me pleasure can bring me back to how I wish to feel on a daily basis.

Imagine being able to tap into your sense of pleasure whenever you desire. It can be both sexual and nonsexual pleasure. You decide. And, remember, things change. You change. It's important to keep checking in with yourself. What may have brought you pleasure last year may have shifted. If you can stay adaptable to the flow of your own life, you are offered such a wonderful perspective. This is an amazing gift.

After all this, where do you go from here?

Well, let's start with your health, in all aspects: mental, emotional, spiritual, physical, nutritional, and relationships.

Where you are succeeding? Where might you need help? Where might you go to get the assistance you need? Who do you need to ask for support?

I know it can be uncomfortable to ask for help. I dealt with feeling scared and insecure for the majority of my life when it came to asking for help, so I didn't ask. In my family of origin, we were stoic and independent. We were taught to take care of our own problems. We didn't talk about them. We sucked it up and dealt with it. Well, how long do we do these things before it takes a toll on us, and we may never even realize it? Can you relate to this, too?

This was a major lesson I learned when I had two small children in diapers, and I thought I could do it all on my own. I could handle it all. I was strong and independent, and I didn't need any stinking help. Until I became ill, stressed, depressed, and at my wit's end. I then did the most brave and vulnerable thing I could ever do: I asked for help. Of course, I thought I was weak, initially. But it was such a godsend to finally get some support. I am grateful for stepping up for myself and getting the help I so desperately needed. It took a lot of courage. It was one of the biggest lessons I learned as an adult.

Asking for help is one of the strongest and most powerful things you can do for yourself. When you try to handle things on your own, especially when you know you need help, it doesn't serve you well. Asking for help serves as a show of internal strength.

Start with these questions:

- "What's stopping me from taking this action?"
- "What is it costing me not to get the help I need?"
- "How would my life be transformed if I changed this right now?"
- "What support do I need to help me with this and who can I ask?"
- "What step could I take that would make the biggest difference now?

When I felt the lowest of lows a few years ago, I completely put my health on the backburner. I ate horribly. I barely exercised. I drank too much alcohol. I slept badly. I was angry and irritable. I was miserable and created misery for my entire family and, really everyone around me. I was numbing out. I buffered my feelings so I didn't have to feel the pain, the hurt, the grief. I just wanted it to all go away. The person I knew became someone I barely recognized. And she frightened me. I imagine she frightened everyone else, as well.

I wasn't embodying the healthy, vibrant woman I'd known myself to be. I allowed all the circumstances, of which I had no control, to take over and take away my power. I craved to find myself again. I wanted to feel well and whole. I made a decision to take my power back. I made a decision to get me back. And, through that process, my sense of self, my self-identity, became healthier and more vibrant than I could've imagined.

In the words of my strength coach and Mentor, Dan John, "If it's important, do it every day." So, I began to do the important things necessary in order to get back on track towards optimal health. I ate better. I ate my veggies. I ate real food (like an adult) and drank water. I stopped drinking. I restarted my stretching and kettlebell strength programs. I danced again. I meditated again. I connected with friends. I slept better. And I asked for help. I went to my doctor to get some much overdue blood work, including a hormonal balance check. I found out that I not only had high familial cholesterol but that I also had almost zero testosterone in my body. As a perimenopausal woman, I still need this important hormone to function normally. Stress was the predominant factor in this hormone imbalance. And after being given my options, I decided to embark on a path of hormone replacement therapy involving a testosterone pellet implant. (Medical Disclaimer: The Content is not intended to be a substitute for professional medical advice, diagnosis, or treatment. Always seek the advice of your physician or other qualified health provider with any questions you may have regarding a medical condition.)

I will tell you that starting the testosterone pellet therapy dramatically changed the course of my life and for the better. This plus the strength training, no alcohol (I have now incorporated a little bit of wine here and there), optimal nutrition (yes, "eating like an adult"), increased sleep hours, and taking care of my mental/ emotional/spiritual/physical/relational health put me on a path in which everything improved. I feel now, as a forty-nine-year-old woman, I am in the very best shape of my life. I have a sense of clarity and purpose. I see that I have absolute autonomy in my choices. I am determined to continue to live in a way that aligns with my values and goals in life. This experience taught me that, life is, indeed, short, and we need to maximize our ability to live our lives with authenticity, passion, and purpose.

How could you take care of yourself differently knowing that this is possible for you?

If you approached this with courage, how could your life change?

I looked for ways in which I could tap into my authentic self and express the passion that I longed to rediscover. I wanted to embrace the things that lit me up. And, I deeply felt that it was my time. It was my time to be the person I wanted to be. And I experienced all that I desired. I am on the journey and I cannot wait to see what I discover next. The beauty of all of this? I am still learning. And the depth of knowledge I am uncovering about myself is astonishing.

What have you always wanted to try? What might light you up? What sounds fun, exciting, adventurous? What might just seem a bit naughty that you are dying to try?

What's stopping you?

You know what? Nothing is stopping you. Except you. You are the only one standing in your way.

Let's do something about that. Right now. Start today. Start with a single step. It will make all the difference.

Chapter 11:

How Do I Keep My Sexy Alive Once I've Found It?

I created a worksheet called "Encompass Your Life" for a client who struggled to get centered and grounded. It is a compass that explores four tenants: love, live, lift, and leap. It's a touchstone to navigate and orient back to center, back to you. It's a brainstorm exercise. I'll share here the one I've done for myself. Have fun with it when you try. Just let it all flow.

Love: "Open Your Heart and Trust the Path Before You." Be true to myself. Be passionate. Be vulnerable. Have self-compassion. Own my value and my worth. Forgive and accept myself.

Live: "Go Forth and Set the World on Fire." Live in the moment. Have balance. Be authentic. Have no regrets. Be here now. Blaze my own trail. Find my soul purpose. Find fulfillment.

Lift: "I Have Done Hard Things Before. I Can Do This." Lift heavy things daily. Be strong as I can for as long as I can. Often and over the long haul. Integrity of body, integrity of spirit. Confidence and fortitude. Strength of mind, strength of body. Lift the veil and have clarity.

Leap: "Sometimes Your Only Transportation Is a Leap of Faith." "Why not" is a great slogan for life. Be afraid and do it anyway. Courage is not an absence of faith; it is the triumph over it. What's the worst that can happen? I fall. I fail. I get back up and start again. I learn. I grow. I change.

As you embrace your sexy self, you learn new things and you build confidence. You experience the power of becoming your authentic self. You may still feel scared; however, you know that now is the time to start taking care of you. Maybe you are going in with caution and testing the waters with your toes in the shallow end. That is awesome. Perhaps you are ready to take a running leap to cannon ball into the deep end. That is awesome, too. And you just might be somewhere in the middle, taking it all in and deciding what level feels comfortable in which to start swimming. Awesome, awesome, awesome. Any way you look at it, you've started. You've begun the process of tapping into what makes you feel sexy, fulfilled, alive. Celebrate this.

Realize that this takes time and effort. Nothing worth having is easy, right? This will take some work. Essentially, it is forming new habits. And, just as with any other new habit, you have to shed old ones to allow the new ones to become ingrained. This must be practiced daily. Just as you need consistent strength training to build up your muscles, you must perform the new habit consistently in order for its muscle to build. Again, it takes time and effort and perseverance.

There's a bigger factor, here, too. And I think it's

important to acknowledge this. In creating these changes, you are letting go of your old self to allow another, transformative version to emerge. You don't like letting go of your identity. You like the feeling of comfort and predictability. As humans, we really do not like change, right? Change is scary. It's looking at the unknown and saying, "No, thanks. I'm just going to stay right here, thank you very much." You'll stay in your comfort because, again, your ego is telling you that danger exists when you go out of the safety and security of what you know. Well, you know what happens when you stay here: you stay small.

Yes, life is predictable and safe, I guess. Although I will argue that staying safe is far from the truth. You may stay in an abusive relationship or an awful work environment. You may enable your adult children. You may not stand up for yourself when someone criticizes you. You don't write that book or decide to go back to college. You are afraid of what might happen to you when you step out and do something new, something out of the norm, even if you know, deep down, that situation on the other side will be better for you. The fears that you conjure up in your own mind are much scarier and more fatalistic than reality. You have a great capacity for creating massive panic and terror, and it only exists because you created it. It becomes a self-fulfilling prophecy if you allow it. You have the ability to change that.

It takes courage and an enormous leap of faith to step into the unknown. When you are brave enough to finally break through the obstacles that you place before you (oh, yeah, all of those barriers are self-made) and get off the hamster wheel of life, it is extraordinary to see what it's like on the other side. That's where the expansive version of yourself lives. That's where the beauty and magic of possibility and opportunity lie. Once you cross over that threshold, you wonder what took you so long.

Anything you decide to take action on begins with a single step. If you wait to become motivated, you will be waiting a long time. The motivation comes out of the doing. You cannot wait to be motivated, you just have to start. And as you are in the "doing" it transforms the experience. Once you're in the process, the momentum takes over and you realize that you want more and more of this feeling. You continue to take those steps, one by one. At some point, you will turn around and reflect on where you've come from. You will surprise yourself to see how far you've traveled. You will see how much you've learned about yourself in that process and that you cannot imagine going back to that point again. You have changed. And you have done so for the better. There is absolutely no desire to return to your old state of being. You like this new you. You love this new you. And you wish to continue to find the things along the way that align with this new way of living.

Why am I telling you all of this? Because it's time. It's time to jump into the beautiful unknown and go after all that your heart desires. It's about reconnecting with yourself and your pleasure, reclaiming your sexuality and feeling sexy again.

Maybe you're ready to talk to your spouse about what you really want out of your relationship. Maybe you are curious about taking this new pole fitness class and you sign up. Maybe you take a half hour every morning to walk in nature and fully take in all the beauty it has to offer. Maybe you begin writing in a journal about this new journey you've embarked on and reflect on where you were, where you are now and where you want to go from here.

Keep coming back to you. Be curious about what resonates with you. And what does not. Say no when you know an opportunity won't serve you. Say yes when it absolutely creates a spark within you. It's not what you think you have to do anymore. It's about what you want to do. It's about what lights you up. It's about what brings you pleasure. It's what brings you back to you.

Explore what is important to you, in every area of your life. Review these questions from time to time and reassess. Be open to flow and new discoveries. What may have worked for you last month may no longer work for you now. It's all okay. There's no wrong choice, here. You always have permission to change your own mind. And that's the beauty, right? You always have choice. Remember these:

- What do you want more of in your life?
- What do you want less of in your life?
- What do you want to eliminate from your life?
- What do you want to enhance in your life?

And when you find out what's most important to you, it must be fed and nurtured. You must practice daily so that it becomes embodied within you.

Love who you are becoming. You are worthy and capable and lovable. It is never too late to start living a life that you desire. Embrace your sexy, confident, gorgeous self. And surprise yourself! In the words of Anne Sexton, be amazed and think, "I am not what I expected."

Chapter 12:

It Starts with a Single Step

Now that you've got the process in the palm of your hands, it's go time, right? You're ready to commit. You're ready to take action. You're ready to do the necessary work. You're ready to reclaim your sexy self and get started right now. You're so excited to begin this program you can barely contain yourself. And you tell yourself that first thing tomorrow morning, you are going to get started. It's going be a new day and a new you. You are pumped.

And then you wake up.

Your kids slept through their alarm, and they're way

late for school, which means you will definitely be late for work. They demand this and that and ask for lunch money and signatures they forgot yesterday. This is the second time this week.

Your husband informs you that he'll be out of town for work next week and he can't help you with his parents' fiftieth anniversary party. Also, he's decided to go take an extra few days to party with his new buddy in Las Vegas.

Your boss wants you to commit to a new work schedule, which includes overseeing the entire department and twenty-five employees. You will definitely have a lot more late nights.

Your parents want you and your family to spend time with them out of state. They are insistent. They say you never spend any time with them, and they want to see their grandchildren before they get too old.

Everything in the universe is going to conspire against you to prevent you from completing this process, including your ego. Your ego will question you relentlessly. You will second guess yourself. You will tell yourself that you don't deserve this. You will tell yourself that you are foolish and everyone else thinks that, too. You will tell yourself that if this happens and you become the woman you truly wish to be, you will be alienated by your friends, your husband will be jealous, your kids will think you're weird, your parents will think you are inappropriate – I mean, who are you to have what you want?

Tell your ego, and all the other phantom naysayers out there, to go take a hike.

Remember something: you are not alone on this journey. Many other women struggle with wanting to feel desirable, loved, seen. They want to embrace the parts of themselves that have been buried. They want to rediscover that sexy self who is yearning to come out and play. And, they need connection. They, too, want to feel that they are not alone.

You also guide others to rediscover their sexy selves regardless of what else happens in their marital, family, or work lives. Life continues to happen around all of you. It keeps moving. Why not engage and allow yourself to become the catalyst for growth? You are paving the way for women to become empowered and transformed and to celebrate their authentic selves.

The only thing standing in your way is you. And you are finally ready. So, what are you waiting for? It starts with a single step. Let's take that step together.

Chapter 13:

Your Pink Wig Moment

In this book, you learned about the Sexy Again Method, those eight steps to feeling sexy again and reclaiming your sexual confidence.

In Step 1, I guided you to assess how you got here at this point in life and how to own your story. Step 2 helped identify your empowered definitions of sexy, dispelled myths and invited the possibilities of how sexy fits into your life now. In Step 3, I taught you how to access these feelings and tap into a sexy-feeling state that is natural and desirable. For Step 4, I supported you to recognize your values, beliefs and goals so that you may become crystal clear on what drives and motivates you in your life. In Step 5, I invited you to acknowledge and transform old patterns that may be holding you back from knowing you deserve to feel sexy. Step 6 paved a way for understanding your power and ability to change your mind-set to get the results you want. You solidified your desire to express your full potential so you can feel sexy and revitalized in Step 7. And in the final step, Step 8, I discussed supportive methods and strategies to keep your sexy alive for good.

It all started with a pink wig. That was my moment. What will be yours? You are ready to reignite your spark. You are ready to reclaim the gorgeous sexy being who lives inside you. My greatest wish for you is to fully and unapologetically connect with your desire, your pleasure and your passion and be the most radiant and authentic version of yourself imaginable.

I look at how my clients Rachel, Debbie and Jenny were so desperate to reclaim a vital part of themselves that they felt were forever lost. I felt the same. They were determined to find their sassy, soulful, lustful, and sexy selves who were just waiting to be rediscovered. I was, too. And as I lived the steps in my program, my

Sexy Again Method was created. I know that it was my method that set my clients on the path toward feeling sexy again and reclaiming their sexual confidence. It was their time to become the version of themselves they so longed to be. They did it. I did it. And you can, too.

Acknowledgments

My childhood was filled with adventure, fantasy, and mystery. The ability to enter a new world from reading words on a page hooked me from a very early age. I had excellent role models who gave me this incredible gift.

My mom, who often read for hours in the bathtub when I was growing up, devoured books. I realized her brilliance as I became an adult and had children of my own (bath time for Mommy!). The ingenious combo of escapism and rejuvenation was definitely not lost on me.

My dad, who'd read anywhere and everywhere at any time, day or night, often finished an entire book in one sitting. If dad wasn't doing a real estate deal or remodeling a house, he was reading, always with one leg crossed over the other. I miss you every day, dad.

And I thank you both for not only instilling this love of reading in me, but in my children. I am grateful beyond words when I see them buried in a book engaged and thoughtful and happy. You helped make that magic happen!

My love for writing came as a natural extension of reading…and calligraphy! I thank my Aunt CJ for this. She gave me my first calligraphy set when I was an adolescent. My desire to practice my fancy letters lead to journal writing which lead to an obsession with needing to put ideas down whenever the mood arose.

Over the years, I collected scraps of paper, Post-It notes, manila folders, volumes upon volumes of journals – all peppered with my ideas, experiences, hopes, and dreams that might, one day, turn into…something! That day has finally arrived.

Carolyn Saarni, PhD, my beloved graduate professor, helped me on my journey toward recovering from my perfectionism and taught me that being good enough was far better than perfect. Admittedly, I am still in recovery; however, she helped pave the way for me to understand that I did not have to stay shackled to thoughts of not being enough. She allowed me to shine, even when I was up to my ears in mud. Thank you, dear Carolyn.

Shelly, Evie, Denell, and Liz, my champions! You always believed in me more than I believed in myself. I needed you to push me to the edge of what I knew I was capable of. And each of you did this exceptionally. You allowed my authentic self to emerge front and center in my life. A million thanks, loves!

I couldn't have survived without the entire Author Incubator team! You so patiently helped me with the technical snafus and the deadlines and the pressures and the insanity of what new authors experience. You all deserve raises!

Ramses, your brilliance in always knowing the right thing to say at just the right moment kept me from getting too close to the ledge. You are my hero!

My magical developmental editor, Ora, you are my favorite mermaid! Girl, we made this happen! Keep dancing in that special way you do. I'm going to name a pole move after you!

Cory, my mystical managing editor, you guided me in finding my true voice and helped craft something of which we are both proud. From the very start, your beautiful soul connected with mine in a way in which I knew we were destined for one another. Love you for your vision, guidance, and loving patience.

Dr. Angela Lauria and The Author Incubator's team, you gave me wings so I could fly. You allowed my dream to finally become realized. And you were right – I will never not be an author again! My servant's heart is in your debt.

Mike, my love, you supported me through a lot of sleepless and cranky times during this process. Thanks for being one hundred percent all-in and supporting my crazy vision. Babe, you might just be a saint! I love you. Cherry and Triple Forever!

Thank you to my Burr and Pembroke children for making your own dinners, doing your laundry, and taking care of the pups while I was tending to my thoughts. You made this process so much easier for me. I love you so much.

A big shout out to my Hebgen Lake cabin cohort for bearing with me during my marathon writing process. It came down to the wire in finishing my manuscript. Your understanding and support got me through that last push. Glad I got to witness the moose with you!

It takes a village to raise a child…and an author. Thank you to everyone who contributed in making this a reality for me. You are loved.

Thank you to David Hancock and the Morgan James Publishing team for helping me bring this book to print.

Thank You!

Hello, beauty! Thank you for reading *Feel Sexy Again: The Ultimate Guide to Reclaiming Your Sexual Confidence*. If you've reached this point of the book, something tells me you're ready to go all the way in order to feel sexy and confident. This is your time!

In deep appreciation to my readers, I'm offering a free gift – the Sexy Again Toolkit – which can be downloaded at www.feelsexyagain.com. This toolkit will help reignite those sparks to light the fire within!

Questions? I can be reached at erica@feelsexyagain.com. And, if you're feeling particularly adventurous and have interest in an intimate retreat experience, please contact me for upcoming locations and details.

This is your time to feel sexy again. It begins today.

xx,

Erica

About the Author

Erica Lemke-Pembroke, MA, is a certified life coach, licensed, specialty-certified New Life Story® wellness coach and sexual confidence coach. Erica has a master's degree in community counseling, with a concentration in marriage and family therapy. She also holds a bachelor's degree in kinesiology and a certificate in gerontology.  She works with clients from a holistic perspective guiding them to connect with themselves – body, mind, and soul.

She has a passion for helping others transform their lives, particularly through dance, strength training and somatic awareness. This led to her work as a functional trainer and dance instructor. Her ability to tap into her sensuality and sexuality early on in her adulthood allowed her to translate her connection to authentic feminine movement with her clients. She's helped countless women understand how to recognize their authentic being and awaken their sensuality.

Erica became certified as a life coach through Coach Training Alliance, and deepened her studies in becoming a licensed, specialty-certified mentor coach and New Life Story® wellness coach through MentorPath®. This furthered her knowledge in neuroscience, strategic coaching, and positive psychology. Combining these disciplines with her passion for keeping one's sensuality and sexuality integral to the whole person, Erica continues her mission of helping women become their most sexually confident selves.

Erica is a Californian, currently living in Utah. She enjoys intimate conversations about sex, adventuring outdoors, dancing daily, writing Haiku poetry and making memorable moments with friends and family.

Printed in the USA
CPSIA information can be obtained
at www.ICGtesting.com
JSHW082358140824
68134JS00020B/2149